ME

of related interest

HITCHCOCK ON HITCHCOCK
edited by Sidney Gottlieb

HITCHCOCK'S FILMS – REVISITED
Robin Wood

Me and Hitch

EVAN HUNTER

faber and faber
LONDON · BOSTON

First published in 1997
by Faber and Faber Limited
3 Queen Square London WC1N 3AU

Photoset by Parker Typesetting Service, Leicester
Printed in England by Mackays of Chatham PLC, Chatham, Kent

A CIP record for this book
is available from the British Library
ISBN 0–571–19306–4

2 4 6 8 10 9 7 5 3 1

This is for Patricia Keim, publicist extraordinaire, who suggested that I write a short piece on me and Hitch.

Me and Hitch:

Evan Hunter with Alfred Hitchcock on the set of *The Birds*.

March 26, 1997 marked ten years since the world première of Alfred Hitchcock's last film, *Family Plot*. My working relationship with him started some forty-one years earlier, when he bought a short story of mine for his then half-hour television show. It ended on May 1, 1963 when I was abruptly replaced as the screenwriter for *Marnie*, his film then in development. What goes around comes around.

Ironically, the short story was titled *Vicious Circle*, and it was originally published in *Real* magazine in March 1953. This was nineteen months before publication of *The Blackboard Jungle*, and I was still writing a *mélange* of short stories and a handful of paperback mystery novels in an attempt to earn a living for myself and my family. The story was about the rise of a small-time hood, culminating in a gangland murder with a surprise twist – just the sort of clever mystery fare Hitch was offering on his enormously popular weekly show.

In its original half-hour format, *Alfred Hitchcock Presents* had premièred on October 2, 1955. Most people who watched the show assumed that he directed each and every episode. In fact, many people believed he also *wrote* the shows' scripts. Hitch did nothing to disabuse anyone of these notions. Years later, when I told one of my sons' friends that I had written the screenplay for *The Birds*, the kid said, 'No, you didn't, Alfred Hitchcock

4

did.' Actually, of the 372 episodes filmed during the lifetime of the television show, Hitch directed only twenty. Bernard Schoenfeld wrote the teleplay for *Vicious Circle*. Paul Henreid directed it.

In both the half-hour format and the hour-long format the show later assumed, Hitch would do a little tongue-in-cheek introduction before the story began, and would then continue with amusing little bits during the commercial breaks. These monologues, coupled with the short cameo appearances he made in all of his films, resulted in him becoming the most highly visible director in the world. I sincerely doubt that many movie-goers today would recognize Steven Spielberg if he walked into a restaurant unannounced. When *Hitch* walked in, *everyone* knew who he was.

I did not know him personally when his Shamley Productions bought my story, and I was not asked to adapt it for television. Joan Harrison, the show's producer, knew my work because by then *The Blackboard Jungle* had been published and the sensational movie based upon it had been released. At the time, however, I'd written only one or two teleplays and no screenplays at all, and I'm sure Joan had no inkling that I was anything but a novelist and short story writer. I'd have been astonished if she'd asked me to write the teleplay of my own story. In fact, the only time I saw the TV version was when it aired for the first time in April of 1957.

I next heard from Hitch, indirectly, in the early part of 1959, when my agent called to say that Shamley had bought a story by one of his clients, and they wanted me to adapt it for *Alfred Hitchcock Presents*. I still had no substantial screenplay or teleplay credits, and I wondered why Joan was willing to take a chance on me. (Hitch later told me he specifically wanted a novelist to adapt this particular story because of its 'internal' nature.) The story was called *Appointment at Eleven*, and it was written by a very good pulp writer named Robert Turner.

The movie *Pulp Fiction* notwithstanding, the expressions 'pulp magazine' or 'pulp writer' may still be unfamiliar. These terms evolved from the fact that the magazines were printed on a yellowish, very grainy grade of paper called 'pulp', in which one could often detect actual wood fibers. These pulps were the forerunners of today's genre novels, specializing as they did in science fiction, detective, sports, adventure, romance and Western stories. The covers of all but the Western, sports and romance pulps were luridly illustrated, and usually depicted a woman in jeopardy. On the science fiction covers, she was scantily clad in a futuristic toga of sorts, and screaming in terror at the approach or embrace of a bug-eyed monster or a mad scientist. On the detective covers, the victim was usually a blonde-haired woman showing a lot of cleavage, her short, tight skirt pulled back over gartered silk stockings. The men threatening her were either unshaven thugs in blue fedoras or long-nailed Orientals in red kimonos. (The covers were always printed in the primary colors.) Some very good writers like Raymond Chandler, Dashiell Hammett and Cornell

Woolrich got their starts in the pulps, but you'd never guess anything of quality was packaged between those sexy front covers and the back covers with their Charles Atlas body-building ads.

Appointment at Eleven is a short story about a young man sitting in a bar, drinking and waiting for 11 p.m. to arrive. The reader doesn't know why. The story is told entirely in the young man's head as alternately he drinks and watches the hands of the clock. At eleven sharp, the lights in the bar dim, and we learn that his father has just been electrocuted at the penitentiary nearby.

This was a difficult story to adapt because it all took place in the lead character's head, in a silent internal monologue. I opened it up by having various people in the bar attempting conversation with him, trying to draw him out. Why do you keep watching that clock, kid? Something going to happen at a specific time, kid? *What* time, kid? And so on. The audience would learn the title when Hitch introduced the show, and this preparation would give me an advantage: *whatever* was going to happen, the audience would already know it would happen at eleven. All I had to do was keep cutting away to the clock and the advancing minute hand for a kind of built-in suspense. Gradually, through casual conversation that becomes inexorably more pointed, we learn that an execution is going to take place down the road tonight, and we learn that the kid has a father, and the father's in jail, and that he's in jail for murder one. When the lights dim and the kid breaks down, we know without question that the man who just got electrocuted was his father, and the shock is almost palpable.

Suspense and shock.

Two of Hitch's trademarks, and I hadn't yet exchanged a single word with him.

I met him for the first time on the set of *The Crystal Trench*, one of the few shows he himself directed for the television series bearing his name. This was sometime during the late summer of 1959. By then, I had written four bestselling novels under my own name, and was on the Coast adapting one of them (*Strangers When We Meet*) for Columbia Pictures. A weekly television series based on the 87th Precinct novels I'd begun writing as 'Ed McBain' three years earlier was scheduled to go on the air that season. Joan Harrison invited Anita, my then wife, and me to the studio to view the final cut of *Appointment at Eleven*, which was to air in November. Watching the film, I discovered to my great surprise that Hitch had abandoned his usual wry introduction, instead stating quite simply that the subject matter of tonight's show was too serious to joke about, and he would let the story speak for itself.

After the screening, Joan took us down to meet him. Since he directed so few of the television shows, his personal appearances on the set were rare, and always occasioned an appreciably higher energy level. There was an unmistakable buzz in the air when we walked down from Joan's office. That day, he was shooting a particularly difficult scene in which an actor was lying under a block of ice, the crystal trench of the title. The ice was resting on a narrow wooden ditch into which the actor had crawled. Another actor was supposed to rub his gloved hand over the ice until the face of the actor below was gradually revealed.

Hitch strolled over from where his people were setting up the scene. Joan introduced us, and he immediately began explaining to my wife the enormous technical problems of lighting the scene from above as well as from inside the trench – somewhat similar to lighting the rain from both front and back in Gene Kelly's famous *Singin' in the Rain* number. At least, that was what I gathered from what I could overhear; all of the conversation was directed at my wife.

Ed McBain is fond of repeating that October 15 is the birth date of great men. On that October 15 I would be thirty-three. Hitch was sixty-two. Anita was all of twenty-nine years old, an attractive, russet-haired woman with green eyes, a warm smile, and a smart New York Jewish Girl sense of humor. Hitch took an immediate liking to her, which was somewhat surprising considering his predilection for glacial blondes. As he showed her around the set, explaining pieces of equipment, introducing her to his cinematographer and his assistant director, the people setting up the shot began to get a bit frantic because the huge block of ice seemed to be melting under the glare of the lights and Hitch still showed no intention of wanting to direct the scene. Finally, after the plaintive words 'Mr Hitchcock, sir, we're ready to go now, sir' had been repeated half a dozen times, he cordially bade us goodbye, and got on with his work.

Two years later, he asked me to write the screen-play for *The Birds*.

The call came from my agent toward the end of August. I thought at first that Joan Harrison wanted me to adapt another story for Hitch's TV show. But no, it seemed Hitch had purchased motion picture rights to a Daphne Du Maurier novella titled *The Birds*, and he wanted me to write the screenplay for the movie he planned to make from it. I told my agent I would have to read the story before I decided. In truth, for the chance to work with Alfred Hitchcock on a feature film, I would have agreed to do a screenplay based on the Bronx telephone book.

The Du Maurier tale was about a Cornish farmer and his wife, whose small cottage is suddenly and inexplicably invaded by birds. There was not a line of dialogue in it. The climactic scene occurs when a huge flock of starlings fly down the chimney and into the room. I told my agent I would like to take a shot at it, and Hitch called me personally that very day.

The first thing he said was that he never wanted to work in Britain again, and certainly did not wish to use as his lead characters an inarticulate farmer and his dreary wife.

'So forget the story entirely,' he said. 'The only elements we'll be . . . '

We'll be!

'. . . using from it are the title and the notion of birds attacking human beings. Other than that, we'll be starting from scratch and building an entirely new story. When can you come out?'

In those days – according to my records, I began work in September 1961 – screenwriters were required to do their actual writing on the Coast. Nowadays, a writer can work wherever he wishes, so long as he delivers the script on time. But back then the habits of a waning studio system were still being honored, more or less, and when a writer was hired he was handed a typewriter, a ream of paper, a secretary, and an office at the studio. A perhaps apocryphal story has William Faulkner asking his producer if he could go 'home' to finish his screenplay, instead of writing in his assigned studio office. The producer thought Faulkner meant home to the Chateau Marmont, where he was staying at the time. Generously, he said, 'Sure, Bill, why not?' Faulkner went directly *home*. To Oxford, Mississippi.

On *Strangers When We Meet*, my agent had negotiated a rented house into the contract, and I'd worked in Santa Monica, on a deck overlooking the Pacific, reporting only once a week to Columbia on Gower Street, for meetings with the director, Richard Quine, and the movie's stars, Kim Novak and Kirk Douglas. The contract I'd signed for writing *The Birds* was for a seven-week minimum term, but Hitch had already told me it might turn into a three-to-four-month project and that I should plan on bringing out my family and placing the kids in school (my notes show that I worked on it for a total of eleven weeks). I told him at once that I could not possibly write in a studio office, and he agreed that I could do the screenwriting itself wherever I chose (in Los Angeles, of course), but that our pre-writing discussions would have to take place in his office at Paramount. We agreed that I would fly out that weekend, get temporarily settled in a hotel, and begin work on Monday morning.

'Bring some ideas,' he said.

I spent my first week on salary . . .

Paying writers 'salaries' was another hangover from the studio's serf system. Nowadays a flat fee is negotiated. But back then, writers were paid so much per week, which might have explained why their presence in LA was deemed necessary. If you're paying a person by the week, you want to know exactly where he is and what he's doing. I got $5,000 a week for writing the screenplay, precisely what I'd got for all my work on *Strangers*. To me, at the time, it seemed a small fortune. (Just before Anita and I left California in November, Hitch asked us to join him and his wife Alma in St Moritz, where they traditionally spent the Christmas holidays. 'You can afford it,' he said, impishly raising an eyebrow to indicate I'd been exorbitantly overpaid.)

Exorbitantly overpaid or not, I reported to work at nine o'clock on the morning of September 18, 1961 and was introduced first to Hitch's personal secretary, a rake-thin, soft-spoken woman named Suzanne Gauthier, and next to Peggy Robertson, a jolly Brit with spectacles, a broad smile, a quick wit, and a razor-sharp mind. Unlike today's politically correct 'assistants', who are really what used to be called file clerks, Peggy was a *genuine* assistant; it

12

was she who inherited the onerous task of firing me from *Marnie* almost two years later.

I only vaguely recall the Paramount offices on Marathon Street. My impression now is that they were similar to but less opulent than those at Universal, where Hitch and I later discussed the *Marnie* screenplay. I remember dark wood paneling and black leather wingback chairs in both offices. I remember Hitch sitting in one of those chairs, clad in a dark blue suit with dark blue socks and white shirt and black tie, his hands clasped over his wide middle, his feet scarcely touching the floor, asking me yet another time to tell him the story so far. I remember in both offices a paneled wall hung with all the awards and plaques and trophies Hitch had garnered in a career then spanning almost four decades.

That morning, the first thing I asked was, 'What do I call you?'

'Why, Hitch,' he said, sounding surprised. 'Everyone else does.'

Which wasn't quite true. I would learn that most people called him what I had heard him called on the *Crystal Trench* set the afternoon the ice was melting: 'Mr Hitchcock, sir.'

The next thing I asked was whether he'd heard the joke about the unemployed actor hired to announce the arrival of celebrity limousines outside the Academy Awards ceremonies at Graumann's Chinese. The actor is immediately warned that Deborah Kerr and John Kerr spelled their last names identically, but Deborah pronounced hers

CAR whereas John pronounced his CUR. Sweating, fearful he will blow his first big opportunity, the actor waits for their limos to arrive. Deborah's limo gets there first, and he announces, 'And here's Deborah CAR's car.' John arrives in his limo, and the actor announces, 'And here's John CUR's car,' and then, enormously relieved, he spots the next limo and announces, 'And here's Alfred Hitchcar's cock!'

Hitch nodded. 'Yes, I've heard it,' he said.

During the first exploratory week of getting to know each other and our individual styles, I arrived in time for breakfast with him in the morning, and we worked together till noon, when he broke for lunch and I went looking for a house to rent. In that first week, I found a house in Brentwood, and Hitch shot down two ideas I'd brought out with me. The first of these was to add a murder mystery to the basic premise of birds attacking humans, an idea I still like. But Hitch felt this would muddy the waters and rob suspense from the real story we wanted to tell. The second was about a new schoolteacher who provokes the scorn of the locals when unexplained bird attacks start shortly after her arrival in town. In the eventual movie, the schoolteacher survived (but not for long) in the presence of Annie Hayworth. In the movie, the town's suspicion and anger surfaces in the Tides Restaurant scene. But Hitch did not want a schoolteacher for his lead; he needed someone more sophisticated and glamorous. Someone like . . .

'Well, Grace, of course,' he told me with a sigh.

'But she's in Monaco, isn't she? Being a prin*cess*. And Cary for the man, of course, whoever or whatever the character may turn out to be. But why should I give Cary fifty per cent of the movie? The only stars in this movie are the birds and me.' And then, as an afterthought, 'And you, of course, Evan.'

(There was never any question in either of our minds, by the way, that the leading role would be a woman's. Instinctively, we recognized that women fear birds more than men do, a psychological truth that later hurt the movie's box office gross and baffled Hitch.)

That first week at Paramount, I came to work wearing jacket and tie. On my second Monday morning, I dressed like all of the other writers on the lot. Slacks, loafers, open throat shirt, V-necked cotton sweater. Hitch wore his customary dark suit, white shirt, black shoes and black tie. Not a sign of disapproval crossed his face as we had our morning coffee and then got down to the serious work ahead of us. But that evening, as I was walking out to my rented red T-Bird convertible parked in a space that already had my name lettered on it, Peggy caught up with me and said, 'Evan, excuse me for mentioning this, but Hitch thinks it might be better if you didn't dress for work quite so casually.'

I drove home along Sunset Boulevard to Brentwood and my rented four-bedroom, two-storey Spanish-style hacienda, with its thick plaster walls and its fireplaces in every room. It was costing me $2,500 a month, merely half of what I was earning each and every *week* I worked on *The Birds*. I had called Anita the night before and told her to pack the kiddies and come on out. Now I mixed myself a drink and sat alone before the fireplace in the downstairs living room and wondered which tie I should wear to work tomorrow morning.

I got there a little early. Sue offered me a cup of coffee, and I stood sipping it in the paneled corridor leading to Hitch's private office, admiring the awards hanging on each side. I heard Sue greeting Hitch, and as he came down the corridor toward me, I thought I detected a quick sweep of his eyes across the sports jacket and tie, an almost imperceptible flicker of approval.

'A lot of wonderful stuff here,' I said, indicating the walls festooned with awards. Hitch nodded dolefully, and put his hand on my shoulder: 'Always a bridesmaid, never a bride,' he said, and I remembered that he'd been nominated for five best-director Academy Awards, including one for *Psycho* just the year before – but had never won any. I was later to learn that the elusiveness of what he considered 'true respect' was the engine that propelled the making of *The Birds*, starting with his having hired me in the first place.

For now, there was a script to write.

'Tell me the story so far.'

These are the words Hitch would say to me every working weekday morning.

'Tell me the story so far.' And every morning, after we'd had our coffee, he would sit back in his big black leather chair with his hands folded over his belly, and I would tell him the story to date, ending with wherever we had left off the afternoon before.

In the beginning, there *was* no story to tell.

Day after day, we grappled with vague ideas and ephemeral notions, doing what the cartoonists call 'snowballing', but the only recurring approach was the kernel of the Stranger-in-Town idea I'd brought from New York. The schoolteacher was gone, of course, an early casualty. What remained was the concept of a woman coming to a strange town which is attacked by birds shortly after her arrival. Do the townspeople have something to hide? Is there a guilty secret here? Do they see this stranger as a messenger of revenge? Are the birds an instrument of punishment for their guilt? All very heavy stuff.

We toyed with this approach for days on end, stopping only for lunch taken in Hitch's office, when he invariably ordered a minute steak, and I ordered tuna and tomato on a hard roll. After lunch, and before we resumed work again, I would take a brisk walk outside the studio while Hitch spent half an hour or so with Peggy and Sue, dealing with the accumulated details of running a production company. It was on one of my solitary strolls that the idea came to me. I take full credit – or blame, as the case may be – for what I suggested to Hitch that afternoon: a screwball comedy that gradually turns into stark terror.

The idea appealed to him at once. I think he saw in it a challenge equal to the one the birds themselves presented. I think, too, that he saw in it a way of combining his vaunted sense of humor with the calculated horror he had used to great effect in *Psycho*. Moreover, the concept had two other things going for it.

We both realized that by the time the movie opened, the audience would know well in advance that birds would be attacking people. If not, then a multi-million dollar promotion and advertising campaign would have been a failure. So there would be a built-in suspense similar to that in *Appointment at Eleven*. Here the title and all the pre-opening hoopla would tell us what would be happening – birds were going to attack – but not *when*. Suspense. And if we could start the audience laughing in the early part of the picture, and then suddenly cause them to choke on their own laughter, the suspense would turn to shock.

During his lifetime, Hitch explained the difference between suspense and shock so often that I'm reluctant to repeat it now. But let me do so hastily.

A meeting is taking place in a boardroom. Men sitting around a table discussing business. We cut away to below the table. We see the businessmen's trousered legs and shoes. Sitting on the floor, unseen by them, is a ticking clock wired to several sticks of dynamite. As the board meeting progresses, we keep cutting away to that ticking clock. Will the bomb be discovered? Or will the dynamite explode when the minute hand and the hour hand are standing straight up? That's suspense.

Same boardroom. Same meeting. Same discussion

of business matters. One difference. We never cut away to the ticking clock and the sticks of dynamite. The audience never knows a bomb is sitting under that table and that it is set to go off at high noon. Suddenly an explosion tears apart the room and everyone in it. That is shock.

Hitch was no stranger to either, and had used both in combination in most of his movies. The difference in *The Birds* would be the goofy humor. Once we got them laughing, we would be leading them down the garden path. And once the early comic scenes turned frightening, then whenever there was a lull between bird attacks, we could hope for a sort of nervous laughter that would lead to further screaming even if we photographed an innocent feather duster.

My own reference points were the black and white comedies I'd grown up with in the forties: Cary Grant and Irene Dunne, Cary Grant and Katharine Hepburn, Cary Grant and Ginger Rogers. Hitch's more personal reference points were the scenes he'd directed between Grace Kelly and Ray Milland, Grace Kelly and James Stewart, Grace Kelly and – yes – Cary Grant. There is no doubt whatever in my mind that as we began discussing the characters who would set our screwball comedy in motion, we were both thinking of Grace Kelly and Cary Grant. This was in September. By November, Grace Kelly had turned into Tippi Hedren and sometime later Cary Grant became Rod Taylor. For now, we were casting platinum.

*

Hitchcock at work with Cary Grant and Grace Kelly
on the set of *To Catch a Thief.*

Grace Kelly goes into a bird shop to buy a myna
bird for a prissy aunt of hers. She intends to teach
the bird some profanities that will shock her aunt.
Cary Grant comes into the shop, mistakes Grace for
a salesperson, and enquires about lovebirds he
wants to buy for his young sister. Ever the prankster,
Grace pretends she does indeed work there, and
Cary goes along with the masquerade, even though
he recognizes her as the madcap socialite daughter
of a prominent newspaper publisher. The brilliant
brittle dialogue between them sets the tone for all
that follows, paving the way for uncontrolled
laughter that pervades until the first of the bird
attacks.

Even though there was, and continues to be, a sometimes wild blend of humor in the 87th Precinct novels – and even though I later wrote two unabashedly comic novels (*A Horse's Head* in 1967 and *Every Little Crook and Nanny* in 1972) – back then in 1961 I was not particularly known for my antic comic flair. Moreover, as I was soon to learn, screwball comedy demands a very special kind of writing that derives more from situation than it does from character. The funny lines in my novels were not gags. The humor came in the innocent utterances of people who didn't know they were saying anything funny. But just as the pulp magazines were the forerunners of today's genre fiction, so were the screwball comedies of the forties the ancestors of today's television sitcoms. Blithely unaware, fast approaching my thirty-fifth birthday and earning five grand a week, I confidently proposed – and Hitch enthusiastically accepted – a concept I had no idea I could actually bring off.

MELANIE
(*solicitously*)
Yes, what was it you were looking for, sir?

MITCH
(*deadpan*)
Lovebirds.

MELANIE
Lovebirds, sir?

MITCH

Yes. I understand there are different varieties, is that true?

MELANIE

Well . . . yes, sir, there are.

MITCH

These are for my sister's birthday. She'll be eleven.
(*lowering his voice*)
Frankly, I wouldn't want a pair of birds that are too demonstrative.

MELANIE

I understand completely, sir.

MITCH

At the same time, I wouldn't want birds that are aloof, either.

MELANIE

Of course not.

MITCH

Do you have a pair that are just friendly?

'When does he realize she's not a salesgirl?'

This from Hitch. Sitting in his big leather chair, eyeing me like a wise old owl. I had not yet written a line of dialogue but I had just told him the story so far, and now he was picking holes in it. This would become our working routine. I would tell him the story, and he would ask questions about it, and I would try to answer them, and then accommodate

22

them. In this way, he edited the script before any of it was actually written, commenting on character development and comic effect in these early scenes of the film. We knew that once the bird attacks started, the audience was ours. But would we be able to keep them sitting still while a Meeting Cute romance between an impetuous young woman and a somewhat staid San Francisco lawyer developed?

From the beginning, Hitch had decided that he would shoot the picture in Northern California. He has shot *Shadow of a Doubt* in Santa Rosa, and was familiar with both the chicken-raising country around Petaluma, and the little coastal town of Bodega Bay. He thought, too, that San Francisco would make a sufficiently sophisticated hometown for The Girl. He invariably referred to the Grace Kelly character (whom I had temporarily named Melanie) as 'The Girl'. Later, when Tippi Hedren was cast for the role, he referred to the actress herself as The Girl. In an odd coincidence, Tippi's then infant daughter was named Melanie. I vaguely remember seeing her at a cocktail party Tippi gave for the Hitchcocks. I had no idea she would grow up to be Melanie Griffith. Neither did Tippi, for that matter.

'Has The Girl called her father yet?'

'Well, no, she hasn't.'

'Well, does he know she's gone up to Bodega Bay to deliver these lovebirds?'

'No, he doesn't.'

'Shouldn't she call him then? So he won't be worried?'

'Yes, she should.'

'Good. You have to remember, Evan, that even though it all goes by too fast for them, they *notice* little things like that and start wondering about them, and stop paying attention to the story.'

In much the same way, Hitch questioned The Girl's *every* move. He said in interviews later (when he was trying to justify the film as a great work of art) that The Girl represented complacency. 'Generally speaking,' he said, 'I believe that people are too complacent. People like Melanie Daniels tend to behave without any kind of responsibility, and to ignore the more serious aspects of life. Such people are unaware of the catastrophe that surrounds us all. The birds basically symbolized the more serious aspects of life.'

This was utter rot, a supreme showman's con.

While we were shaping the screenplay, there was no talk at all of symbolism. There *was* talk about character depth, but Hitch's real concerns about the shallowness of the people we'd chosen did not emerge until after I'd delivered the first draft and he'd solicited opinions from everyone but his barber. The inherent problem, of course, was that the characters in a screwball comedy *have* no depth. They merely represent conflicting attitudes. We were trying to tell a story lighter than air. The irony was that the terror later comes from the air. As far as I was concerned, everything that preceded that first gull hitting Melanie on the head was pure gossamer.

Hitch had a different agenda. Hitch wanted respectability.

In his book, *Hitchcock, The Making of a Reputation* –
published thirty years after the movie had its first
press screening at the Museum of Modern Art in
New York City – Robert E. Kapsis wrote, '*The Birds*
represents the first, the most ambitious, and certainly the most expensive project the filmmaker
undertook for the purpose of reshaping his reputation among serious critics.'

Had I but known.

I once asked him why he'd hired me for the film.

He replied, 'I make it my business to know what's
going on, Evan.'

I had no idea what he meant.

He later told a journalist, 'Hunter wasn't the ideal
screenwriter. You look around, you pick a writer,
hoping for the best.'

I suspected at the time that he'd hired me to 'open
up' the basically internal Du Maurier story, just as
I'd done earlier with *Appointment at Eleven*. I
suspected that he'd hired me because he recognized
in the 87th Precinct novels someone who knew how
to write suspense. It never occurred to me that he
was hiring me because I was the man who'd written
The Blackboard Jungle. Never mind the later movie
with its skewed emphasis on juvenile delinquency.
The book itself had received serious critical apprai-
sal. In Hitch's mind, I had respectability.

Tell that to my kids.

In August 1961, a month before I went out to work on
The Birds, my oldest son Ted had just turned eleven.

His twin brothers, Mark and Richard, were nine years old. The house I'd rented in Brentwood was the closest thing to a city street they'd ever seen. I was born and raised in New York, and knew its mean streets, and had learned, among other things, how to make rings from peach pits. You scrape the pit on the sidewalk until it is flat on each side. You round out the sharp edges the same way. Then you carve out the center with a sharp knife. *Voilà, une bague!* The things you learn when you're underprivileged.

There were no sidewalks on our Brentwood street. I taught the kids how to make peach-pit rings on the rough surface of the concrete driveway sloping up to our garage, where Anita's rented station wagon sat alongside my red T-Bird convertible. A high-priced entertainment lawyer named Harold Berkowitz lived in the house next door. Across the street lived Norman Katkov, who'd written a powerful novel titled *Eagle at My Eyes*; coincidentally, he also wrote the first-draft screenplay for *Strangers When We Meet*, before he was replaced by me. My kids were enrolled in the Bellagio Road Elementary School. When they told the other kids I was writing a screenplay for Alfred Hitchcock, none of them blinked an eye. Small wonder in a school where Burt Lancaster's wife was president of the Parent–Teacher Association.

Work progressed.

Day by day, I told Hitch the story so far.

I realize now that I was uncomfortable with the character of Melanie Daniels from minute one. I

A choice of heroines: Melanie Daniels (Tippi Hedren)
or Annie Hayworth (Suzanne Pleshette).

would have much preferred a frightened schoolteacher as my heroine. Even the schoolteacher who
survived as Annie Hayworth wasn't much to my
liking. Suzanne Pleshette later tried to rescue her
from jilted spinsterhood, but the character never did
work, not in our discussions, not on paper, and
eventually not on the screen. It didn't help that
Hitch dressed this beautiful woman like a grocer's
wife, lighted her badly, and shot her from the most
unflattering angles. Three minutes after we'd been
introduced on the set, the first words Suzanne said
to me were, 'The blonde, he gives a mink coat. Me,
he gives wedgies and a house dress.' I fell in love
with her at once.

'The blonde, he gives a mink coat': Hitchcock
with Tippi Hedren.

'Me he gives wedgies and a house dress': Hitchcock
with Suzanne Pleshette.

Early on in our discussions, Hitch and I tried to justify why a man of Mitch Brenner's age was still effectively living at home with his mother and kid sister. We had him practicing criminal law in San Francisco and then commuting to Bodega Bay on weekends, an odd thing for an eligible young bachelor to be doing. It became Annie's burden to define the mother's possessive behaviour in a heart-to-heart talk with Melanie, who at this point in the script seemed to be in more danger from Lydia Brenner than from any of the still quiescent birds.

In the script as it evolved, this emphasis on the 'deeper' aspects of our leading characters came only after the initial bird attack, as if to signal no more fun and games, kiddies, the *real* show is about to start. Moreover, not only would we be dealing with rampant birds, we'd also have on our hands a jealous widowed woman clinging to her only son. Jessica Tandy played the part of the mother like a deer caught in a truck's headlights, one of the few bad performances she ever gave in her life. One of the lines I wrote for Annie was, 'Lydia's not afraid of losing her son, you see. She's only afraid of being abandoned.' Watching Ms Tandy sleepwalking, I got the feeling that she really *had* been abandoned. By the script *and* by the director. But Hitch liked that line. It was later expanded upon in a terrible scene that handed Lydia's entire theme of 'being abandoned' to none other than our ditzy screwball socialite.

When I first suggested 'Screwball Comedy Becomes Terror', Hitch should have said, 'That is the worst idea I have ever heard in my life. Let's

Jessica Tandy: like a deer caught in a truck's headlights.

move on.' Instead, we marched ahead confidently, blithely trying to graft upon Du Maurier's simple tale of apocalyptic terror a slick story about two improbable lovers confronted with an even more improbable situation – birds attacking humans.

The trouble with our story was that *nothing* in it was real. In real life, birds *don't* attack people and girls don't buy lovebirds to shlepp sixty miles upstate for a practical joke. Hitch had bought a bizarre novella about plain people attacked by the gentlest of creatures. He had then hired a realistic novelist from New York to change these people into the sort of beautiful, sleek, sophisticated characters Hitch himself enjoyed seeing on the screen, the Cary Grants and Grace Kellys of the world. Even if the

Tippi Hedren: no Grace Kelly.

script had worked – which it didn't – Tippi Hedren and Rod Taylor were no Grace Kelly or Cary Grant.

But Hitch never gave it an honest shot.

I can remember the morning I related the scene toward the end of the film where Melanie goes up to

Rod Taylor: no Cary Grant.

the attic to investigate some odd sounds and is attacked by what appears to be an entire aviary. I had asked Hitch early on how much latitude I could have in the bird attacks. He told me to write whatever I wished and then let him worry about getting it on film. In what I visualized as the movie's penultimate attack, I had a mixed assortment of birds in that attic, starting with an owl who sits peering at Melanie in the dark, and then spreads his enormous wings and comes flying straight into her face.

'We see all kinds of birds here,' I told him. 'Eagles, hawks, owls, crows, gulls, small birds, big birds, *all* of them, Hitch! This is where we realize this isn't just some finches coming down the chimney or some gulls attacking a gas station, this is the whole damn bird *population*, this is a united attempt to annihilate the human *race!*'

Hitch looked at me with a blank expression I would later come to recognize as his personal 'take'.

'Why does she go up to the attic?' he asked.

'Because she hears sounds up there.'

'Bird sounds?'

'No. The sound of something falling, or dribbling down, sifting down. Actually, it's plaster. She's hearing plaster falling, but she doesn't know what it is. So she goes to investigate.'

'Why doesn't she wake Mitch?'

'She tries to. She can't wake him. He's dead asleep.'

'So, as I understand this,' Hitch said, 'we've just come from the Tides Restaurant where the gulls have devastated the place, and we've just had a massive attack on the house here, with Mitch fighting off birds who try to come in the windows and doors, and now Melanie hears some strange sounds and she goes to *investigate*? Is she daft?'

I said, 'Well.'

'Don't worry,' he said, 'we'll take the curse off it. Just have her check everything in sight till she's satisfied nothing's wrong. *Then* she gets hit.'

FULL SHOT – MELANIE
As she goes through the house, checking. She stops in the entry hall, plays the flashlight over the furniture piled against the door. Everything seems all right. She goes into the kitchen, again checks the door, and then plays the beam on the boarded windows. Satisfied, she

goes down the corridor outside the bedrooms. She opens
the first bedroom door, enters, goes to the windows,
plays the beam on them. Everything's all right. She
comes out into the corridor again, opens the second
bedroom door, again checks the windows, and leaves.

FULL SHOT – MELANIE
Climbing the steps to the attic. She stops outside the
first door upstairs, opens it, goes into the room, plays the
light on the windows. Nothing. She comes out into the
corridor, goes to the second bedroom, opens the door,
enters, walks to the windows. They are boarded securely.
She is starting back toward the door when she stops.

CLOSE SHOT – MELANIE
Looking.

CLOSE SHOT – THE FLOOR
A pile of chipped and broken plaster.

MEDIUM SHOT – MELANIE
Turning the flashlight up toward the ceiling.

CLOSE SHOT – THE CEILING
A huge hole in it, showing a moonlit sky outside.

CLOSE SHOT – MELANIE
Turning her eyes from the ceiling, determination on her
face. And suddenly, her eyes open wide.

CLOSE SHOT – AN OWL
Sitting in the darkness, staring at her.

That is how the scene reads in the final script. Which
I was now almost ready to write.

The attack in the attic.

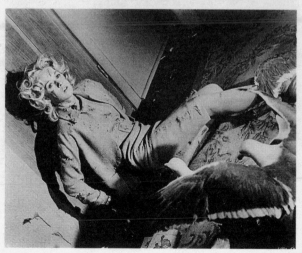

'Dinner in the kitchen with Alma and Hitch' was considered a singular honor. I had been so informed by Ernest Lehman, who had written the original screenplay for *North by Northwest* and who had graciously and generously welcomed Anita and me to Los Angeles with a cocktail party shortly after she arrived with the kids. With our discussions on the script almost at an end, Hitch casually asked if Anita and I would care to join him and Alma for dinner that Saturday night. 'Just the four of us,' he said. 'Around the kitchen table.'

We arrived at seven-thirty, and Hitch introduced us to Alma, his wife since December 1926. In early October of 1961, they had been married almost as long as I'd been on earth. Alma was a successful film editor when he met her and later she worked on many of his films, receiving adaptation, screenplay and continuity credits. A tiny, animated woman, she fluttered about like a bird herself, amiable and warm, cordial and welcoming. Hitch asked us what we'd care to drink. Anita wasn't much of a drinker. She asked for a white wine spritzer. I asked for a Canadian Club and soda.

Hitch stood staring at me. His classic take.

Then he said, 'Well, Evan, I'm afraid we don't *have* any Canadian Club.' Beat. 'But we're very well appointed otherwise.'

Before dinner, he proudly exhibited his wine cellar to us. Anita innocently pulled one of the bottles partly out of its rack, and turned it to read the label. Hitch was aghast.

'Anita,' he said, 'do you know what you just *did*?'

Patiently, he went on to explain that turning the bottle caused the sediment to do something or other – again this was all addressed to Anita, and I caught very little of it.

Scolding her, a twinkle in his eye, he said, 'You must never do that again.'

He never took us into the wine cellar again. But the next time we went to the house, a bottle of Canadian Club was sitting on the bar.

I followed Hitch into Peggy Robertson's office.

'Peggy,' he said excitedly, 'wait till you hear how we're going to end the film. Sit down, sit down. Evan, tell her the ending. Listen to this, Peggy.'

Reciting the day's work to Hitch's assistant had also become something of a ritual. It was not as laborious as the morning recitations, because it did not involve weeks of work but only that day's story developments. On that particular day, we had mapped out the final attack in the film. Now, at a little past five in the afternoon, Peggy sat and listened.

I began by explaining that after the attack on Melanie in the attic, and a brief scene during which Lydia reveals her fears and vulnerability, they all come out of the house into that sort of eerie half-light before dawn. All the birds have gone. They get into Melanie's convertible and begin driving away from the house.

'This is where we see the terrible devastation in the town,' I said. 'This is where we realize the attack on the farmhouse wasn't just an isolated incident. This is a war zone . . . '

Birds are everywhere, in the trees, on the telephone wires, perched on an overturned school bus and a derelict barge. Victims are lying in the road and in open shop doors. Merchandise and household goods are strewn everywhere. From behind smashed windows, we see frightened faces peering out. The car moves cautiously ahead through thousands of birds waiting, waiting. There is a clean stretch of road ahead. 'Here we go,' Mitch says, and rams his foot down on the accelerator. Instantly, thousands of birds take wing. The road is winding and twisting, the same road Melanie negotiated into town at the beginning of the movie. But the birds fly in a straight line, relentlessly attacking the car, slashing at . . .

'The car is a convertible, remember? With a canvas top. From inside the car, we see a single beak slashing at the top, letting in light, and then another slash, and another, letting in more and more light until finally . . . '

CLOSE SHOT – LYDIA

LYDIA
(*almost in prayer*)
Dear God . . . dear God . . . please, please, what have we done? Please.
(*and then, in anger at the roof and the birds*)
Can't they leave us alone?
(*shrieking it*)
LEAVE US ALONE!

MEDIUM SHOT – THE CAR INTERIOR
All the passengers, as the roof suddenly rips back.

40

FULL SHOT – THE BIRDS
From inside the car, hovering over it the moment the roof tears back.

'This is too much for Melanie. She screams and turns her face into Lydia's shoulder. The car races around curve after curve . . . '

I had Peggy now, and I was enjoying myself.

'. . . the canvas top streaming tattered ribbons behind it. But they can't shake the birds flying above. Until finally, the road ahead straightens, and the small car begins to outdistance them. Another flock attacks from the side of the road, but the car speeds into them and through them . . . '

CLOSE SHOT – LYDIA

LYDIA
We're losing them.

CLOSE SHOT – MITCH
Only a nod, his face streaming tears.

TWO SHOT – CATHY AND MITCH
Side by side on the front seat.

CATHY
Mitch? Will they be in San Francisco when we get there?

MITCH
(*grimly*)
I don't know, honey. I don't know.

'. . . and the car rides into the sun coming up over the crest of the hills, racing further and further into an uncertain distance.'

Peggy was silent for a moment. Then she said, 'Bravo.'

Smiling, Hitch nodded and said, 'Yes.'

Later on, he remembered his agenda.

I wrote the screenplay on a portable Smith-Corona (my own) in a small bedroom on the second storey of the house. As I typed away, birds chirped in the big oak tree outside my window. Now that our discussions had ended, I rarely spoke to Hitch. Instead, he called Anita every morning, and chatted with her on the phone, asking how the children were doing in school, asking if she'd yet found a tennis partner or a good hairdresser; warm and genuine concerns for he was truly fond of her. Never once did he ask her how the screenplay was coming along. Nor on our frequent social outings did he ever ask me how things were progressing. He offered me the respect of a fellow professional. He knew I was working. He knew I would yell if I ran into any problems.

I had no problems.

And I foresaw none.

One Saturday, he took us to Santa Anita. As we entered the track, he took out his billfold and handed Anita a hundred-dollar bill . . .

'This is for you, Anita.'

. . . and handed me a hundred dollars as well.

42

'And this is for you, Evan.'

'What for?' I asked.

'Why, to bet.'

I explained that if we accepted the money we'd feel no pain if we lost, and if we won we'd feel obliged to turn over the winnings to him. Hitch did his straight-faced take.

'In that case, give it back to me,' he said, and snatched the bills from our hands.

He told me he felt he was entering the Golden Age of his creativity. He told me *The Birds* would be his crowning achievement.

But after he'd had too much wine, he would take Anita's hand between both of his, and pat it, and tell her he was nothing but a big fat slob.

He called Anita one morning to ask what time we'd be meeting for dinner together that night. Baffled, she said, 'I didn't know we'd made plans, Hitch. I'm sorry, but we're busy.'

There was a stunned silence.

Then Hitch, enraged, shouted, 'What the hell are Alma and I supposed to do?'

We canceled our plans.

On Halloween night, they arrived to pick us up in a limo. Hitch himself got out, came to the front door, and rang the doorbell. My son Ted answered his ring.

'Which one are you?' Hitch asked.

'I'm Ted.'

'Happy Halloween, Ted,' he said, and handed

him a personalized and autographed copy of his recently published collection, *Alfred Hitchcock's Haunted House*. 'Where are your brothers?'

He waited on the doorstep while Ted went to fetch them. Sorting out the twins, he handed a second similarly inscribed copy to Mark and yet another to Richard.

'Happy Halloween,' he said. 'Now would you please tell your parents we're here?' And went back to the car.

On a Tuesday morning, November 6, there was a noisy gathering of birds in the back-yard. Watching them through the window, from the desk where I was writing the final scene of the film, I figured that somehow they had learned what Hitch and I were up to and were coming to get us.

The phone rang some five minutes later.

It was Hitch calling to report to Anita that the hills behind his Bellagio Road house were on fire.

'Well, don't worry,' she told him. 'Just call the fire department.'

'Anita,' he said – very patiently, considering that this was to become the enormous brush-fire that burned down hundreds of homes in Bel Air and threatened to leap Sunset Boulevard to create a true holocaust – 'Anita, you don't understand. *Everything* is on fire. Alma and I are going to carry all of our things down to the wine cellar. Or do you think we should throw them in the pool?'

'What things?' Anita asked.

'Our silver, Alma's fur coats . . . '

'Well, I wouldn't throw the *coats* in the pool,' Anita said.

'Anita, please be serious. We're thinking of moving into a hotel.'

'Do you think we should leave *here*?'

'Go take a look outside,' he said.

We took a look outside. All of our neighbours were on the street, peering toward the end of the block, where flames were already edging their way over the brow of the hill.

Hands on his hips, Norman Katkov said, 'We may not be much on story out here, but we sure know how to do spectacle.'

At the elementary school not far from Hitch's house, a television reporter was interviewing children who were being evacuated, among them my three sons.

'What's your name?' the reporter asked Mark.

'Mark Hunter.'

'What do you think of this fire, Mike?'

'Mark.'

'What do you think about the school being evacuated, Mark?'

'To tell the truth,' Mark said, 'I was *hoping* it would burn down.'

Cars were backing out of garages. Birds were everywhere in the air. People were fleeing with their valuables. In this house we were renting, there were none of our own valuables. We packed some clothes, my typewriter, and the almost finished script of *The Birds*, locked the front door, got into

45

the two cars, and drove across Sunset Boulevard to the high school.

That night, we returned to the house.

The fire had not done any damage on our street.

That week, I finished the first draft screenplay.

Dear Mr Hunter:

This is to confirm that today, Friday, 10th November, 1961, you have completed the screenplay of *The Birds*. However, Mr Hitchcock will require your services in connection with *The Birds* for an additional two weeks – probably sometime in January 1962.

Sincerely,
Peggy Robertson
Assistant to Mr Hitchcock

In a five-page letter from Hitch dated November 30, 1961, after he'd gone over the first draft a couple of times and shown it to some eight or nine of his technical and production personnel, he went into elaborate detail on the various problems he and his people had found.

The problem most frequently cited among them was that Melanie and Mitch seemed 'insufficiently characterized'. The next problem – and this seemed particularly to concern Hitch – was that there were too many 'no-scene scenes' in the script. 'By this I mean that the little sequence might have narrative value but in itself is undramatic. It very obviously lacks shape and it doesn't within itself have a climax as a scene on the stage might.' He went on to detail these scenes at great length: a scene between Melanie and her father in his newspaper office; two scenes in Bodega Bay where Melanie goes to buy some temporary overnight clothes and later tries to rent a room at a fully booked hotel; and lastly, a scene inside the local church, where she runs into Mitch again. None of these survived the final draft, none was in the completed film.

In a long and masterfully detailed paragraph, Hitch went on to suggest how we could begin foreshadowing the bird attacks from the very beginning of the film. Lastly, he wondered whether we shouldn't start thinking about giving the script a stronger thematic structure, and wrote, 'I'm sure we are going to be asked again, and again, especially by the morons, "Why are they doing it?"'

On December 14, I sent fifty-two revised pages to him, among them a new scene between Melanie and Mitch, during which they try to understand what's happening. The scene takes place after Lydia has gone off to the Fawcett farm. It is light-hearted at first, echoing the screwball comedy that had opened our story. Melanie proposes that this all must have started with a malcontent sparrow preaching revolution, attracting other sparrows to his cause, inciting them to unite, his followers growing larger in number until now they were a force to contend with. They both laugh at this absurd notion, and then fall silent. Seriously, Mitch suggests that perhaps the birds are merely hungry; it's been a bad summer, no berries or nuts in the burned-out hills. Everything is deathly still. They

47

realize it is the same lull that occurred yesterday, before the finches attacked. They try to joke about the attacks again, but now the humor falls flat and there is the chill of horror to Melanie's words when she says those finches came down that chimney in fury – as if they wanted everyone in the house *dead*.

MELANIE
I'm frightened, Mitch.

MITCH
No, no . . .

MELANIE
I'm frightened and confused and I . . . I think I want to go back to San Francisco where there are buildings and . . . and concrete and . . .

MITCH
Melanie . . .

MELANIE
. . . everything I know.

She looks up at him suddenly.

CLOSE SHOT – MELANIE

MELANIE
Damn it, why'd you have to walk into that shop?
(*they kiss suddenly and fiercely*)

Which is how Lydia happens to discover them in an embrace when she drives back after finding Dan

Fawcett with his kitchen a shambles and his eyes pecked out.

From what I understand, Hitch shot this scene. But he never used it, and its absence is sorely felt.

Without this scene, no one in the film ever *really* questions why the birds are doing this, and if our leading characters aren't even looking for answers, then the audience will *demand* them. Moreover, without the only scene in the picture that would have shown our screwball lovers finally kissing seriously and passionately, there is no climax – you should pardon the expression – to all their nutty sparring and running around. We haven't the faintest clue as to why Mitch is suddenly calling her 'darling' for the rest of the film. We are utterly baffled.

It all goes by too fast for them, Evan. But in this case, it didn't go by too fast at all. It simply wasn't there.

Hitch's response to my revisions came a week later, in a four-page letter dated December 21. He ended with the words, 'Well, Evan, there it is – I pray I am not giving you too much to think about over the Christmas holidays. Perhaps it would be nicer if you took this letter and put it under the tree and then on Christmas Eve you could pull it out and say "Oo look, a present from Hitch".'

P. S. People are still asking 'Why did the birds do it?'

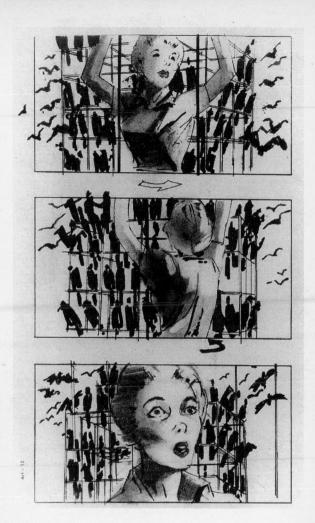

BODEGA
SCHOOL
YARD.

237 - crows fly away from playgound. equips at sound
of children running.

matte

#38 crows over school.

matte

crows head for children.

near
Bodega
School.

Melanie — Run — Run.

Children (foregrnd against Sodium Screen) Backgrnd
Bodega school with michelle and 2 or 3 children.

continuation of 440. Melanie runs past camera

December 27, 1961

Dear Peggy:

It was good talking to you today, and I shall look
forward to seeing Hitch on January 4th. At that
time I'll discuss the further revisions he wants in
the script . . .

January 17, 1962

Dear Hitch:

I am enclosing herewith the final version of *The
Birds*, incorporating the changes we discussed
when you were in New York. The two biggest
changes in the script were the scene between Annie
and Melanie, and of course, the meeting in the
Tides. You will find in this scene an alarmist, a
pacifist, and various other types. On the whole, I

54

think it plays very well and serves our needs beautifully.

I have carefully gone over each of the bird attacks and the reactions of our principal characters following these attacks. I honestly do not feel we now have a simple reaction of terror. It seems to me that the characters now are changing throughout the entire length of the screenplay and that each change is a logical one following the change before it. I am glad we decided to introduce a romantic interest between Mitch and Annie. This seems to provide more dramatic strength and helps to answer a great many questions regarding Lydia as well. You will notice that I have gone through the script and tightened dialogue wherever I felt it was redundant, vague, and unnecessary. I am rather pleased with what we now have, and I shall be anxious to hear your reactions.

I hope to hear from you soon. Please give our love to Alma.

What I did not know was that Hitch had already solicited comment on the script from Hume Cronyn, an actor who had received 'adaptation' credit on two of Hitch's previous films, *Rope* in 1948 and *Under Capricorn* in 1949. Mr Cronyn's comments had arrived before my revisions. In his letter of January 13, 1962, he suggested that there was 'still room for improvement in the development and relationship of the principal characters. The implied arrogance, silliness, and selfishness of the early Melanie may need heightening, so that the change to consideration, responsibility, and maturity are more marked – and more enduring.'

He was merely the first who – without my knowledge or consent – stuck his finger in the concept and his foot in the whorehouse door.

'I ask you, Evan, how can anyone have respect for a man who earns his living by putting makeup on his face?'

On January 29, 1962, Peggy Robertson wrote to tell me that the mimeo'd final script of *The Birds* would be ready that week.

'Would you like to return the leather-bound copy Hitch gave you so that we can have the book-binders insert this final version?'

My leather-bound copy of the mimeo'd final script included the last seven pages of the screen-play, detailing the car moving through the deva-stated town and the final harrowing attack of the birds on the small canvas-topped convertible.

Hitch never filmed those pages.

Back in 1962, it was an axiom of the trade that when a writer finished his screenplay, the best thing he could do for all concerned was get lost. This has changed to some extent, but I recently heard a famous director tell a group of professional screen-writers that a director should of *course* be willing to sit down and discuss with a writer the 'intent' of his script. But when it came to the actual shooting of the picture, there could be 'only one captain of the ship' and the writer should stay away from the set and the actors. I was on location while *The Birds* was shooting in Bodega Bay, and later on while Hitch was filming some interiors on the Universal lot in Los Angeles. But although I was there by invitation, in a sense I was there merely by accident: Hitch had hired me to write his next picture, *Marnie*, based on the novel by Winston Graham, and we were discussing our approach to the film.

The day Anita and I arrived on the set, they were rehearsing the scene outside the Tides Restaurant, where a gull swoops down on the service station attendant pumping gasoline, knocking him down and causing him to drop the hose. A man lighting a cigar drops his match into the stream of flowing

The burning gasoline station.

gasoline and the subsequent explosion attracts a squadron of gulls who dive-bomb the town.

(After I saw the film, it always amazed me that no one ever questioned how Hitch had got the gulls to *do* that. Was he up there in an airplane, shouting '*Now*, boys!' into a megaphone? It never occurred to anyone that the birds were animated cel by cel onto footage of the gasoline station burning below. It was merely accepted that somehow Hitch and his bird-trainer had managed to get those gulls to peel off on cue.)

Hitch shook hands with me and then embraced Anita cordially. Rod Taylor was sitting in a director's chair with his name lettered on the back of it, watching the rehearsal. Hitch turned to him, and with elaborate Cockney disdain, said, 'Mr Taylor, can't you see there's a *lady* on the set? I'm sure you'd like to give her your chair, wouldn't you?'

Rod leaped to his feet at once.

In an aside loud enough for Rod and every bird in northern California to hear, Hitch whispered to me, 'Cattle, Evan. They're all cattle.'

The stuffed gull on its guy wire swooped down and hit the service station attendant on the head yet another time.

Every day we would ride in a limo from San Francisco to the Bodega Bay location, leaving the Fairmont Hotel very early in the morning. School children lined the roads north, holding up makeshift signs lettered with the words 'MR HITCHCOCK, PLEASE STOP!'

Hitch always directed the driver to stop the car.

He spent fifteen minutes, sometimes half an hour graciously signing autographs.

We discussed *Marnie*.

We discussed *Marnie* on the sixty-mile ride to and from location. We discussed *Marnie* during lulls in the shooting and during lunch and during dinner every night. We discussed *Marnie* interminably.

There was one scene in the book that bothered me.

'Which scene is that?' Hitch asked. He knew which scene it was.

'The scene where he rapes her on their wedding night.'

'Oh, don't worry about that,' Hitch said. 'That'll be fine.'

I knew it wouldn't.

There was no doubt in my mind that Hitch had decided to film the Winston Graham novel only because he saw in it a vehicle for Grace Kelly. Who better to play a compulsive thief who also happens to be frigid because of a childhood trauma? Grace Kelly committing burglaries? Grace Kelly riding a horse after each theft? Grace Kelly being blonde and elegant and glacial and elusive? Grace Kelly being Grace Kelly? Perfect.

In fact, when I asked him who would be playing the lead, he winked and mouthed the single word 'Grace'.

Apparently he didn't mouth it softly enough.

Perhaps because I had behaved so responsibly while writing in Brentwood, or perhaps because Hitch was shooting and didn't want me underfoot, he raised no objection to my writing the *Marnie* screenplay in New York. When I got off the plane at Kennedy, a horde of reporters and photographers rushed to the gate. I wondered who it was they were there to meet.

'Mr Hunter?' one of them asked.

'Yes?'

They were there to meet me.

'Is it true that Grace Kelly will be starring in Hitchcock's next film?'

'I don't know,' I said. 'You'll have to ask him.'

'Did he tell you she'd be playing the lead in *Marnie*?'

'You'll have to ask him.'

'Does that mean yes?'

'It means you'll have to ask him.'

I don't know who they asked.

But on March 20, the *New York Times* reported that Princess Grace would be coming out of retirement to play the leading role in *Marnie*, and the story was reported in the British press the very next day. The Prince and his loyal subjects obviously disagreed. Hitch's preferred star withdrew from negotiations on the film, and Tippi Hedren got the role by default.

Meanwhile, back at the ranch . . .

Unknown to me, Hitch had already sent the script of *The Birds* to an old friend of his, V. S. Pritchett, a short story writer who used to be the book review editor for the *New Statesman*.

On March 16, before the *Times* story broke – and while I was busily dissecting the Graham novel scene by scene and beginning my own research into banking (Marnie robs banks) and big business (she robs businesses, too) and psychiatry (she's a little nuts, you see) – Pritchett wrote back. He said that audiences of *The Birds* would 'get the impression that they are in two different stories – in this case a light comedy and a terror tale – that do not weld together'.

While Hitch pondered this startling revelation that merely defined the entire approach to the film, he asked me to take another look at the final scene, with an eye toward giving it a deeper meaning and a stronger purpose.

In a letter to Hitch dated March 30, 1962, addressed to the Fairmont in the hope that I would still catch him there, I suggested some locations that Robert Boyle (Hitch's production designer, who'd first begun working with him on *Saboteur* in 1941) might want to look at for *Marnie* and promised that the revised last scene of *The Birds* would be coming Hitch's way the following week. 'I want to tell you,' I wrote, 'that it's a little difficult to be poetic when the roof of an automobile is slowly being shredded to bits by attacking birds.'

I wrote further:

My session with our psychologist proved most rewarding. I now understand a great many of the things happening in the book (Winston Graham was either using a case history, or else was intuitively correct) and can cope with our dear Marnie very well indeed. You will be interested to learn that our psychologist felt the ending we worked out – concerning Marnie's trauma – was a *more* valid one than the one in the book. So it's full speed ahead with our drunken sailor and our intervening mother and, oh, all sorts of Oedipal undertones and overtones.

I am picking up a book on screen memory this afternoon. I understand the phenomenon quite well in its simplest terms, but I want to go into it a little more deeply just in case I decide to explain it to an audience at some point in the picture. In any case, I learned some exciting things which will provide us with a *double* twist on the trauma. I'm not anticipating any trouble at all.

Famous last words.

There is a trauma.

Dream work reveals what appears to be the true memory of what happened long ago.

But the revelation is a false one.

A screen memory (not as in *movie* screen but as in something behind which one retreats to change one's clothes) is a *false* memory of the trauma. It hides the *real* memory which the traumatized victim cannot face. I did indeed explain all this to an audience, in highly dramatic scenes Hitch never used in his movie. In the picture that was finally made from Jay Presson Allen's screenplay, for which she received sole credit, Hitch discarded the complicated screen memory concept altogether, opting instead for a simpler bargain-basement explanation of Marnie's compulsive thievery and frigidity.

It was the frigidity that would cause the problem later on.

I delivered the final pages of *The Birds* on April 2, 1962, the day after my twin sons' tenth birthday. In my accompanying letter, I wrote:

I have taken the liberty of transposing several of your outlined shots in order to present the menace as a growing and cumulative one. For example, I didn't feel the shot showing 'only a few gulls' in the road would cause the consternation it did in your outline. Considering the number of birds they have already seen, their reactions to those few seem a bit excessive. Too, I feel it necessary to provide a trapped feeling when they approach the hundreds of gulls sitting in the middle of the road. In other words, there is no choice; they are literally surrounded and *must* go through the center of the waiting birds.

Concerning our 'poetry', as I told you in my earlier letter, it was a little difficult to wax literary when the roof and the whole damn world are falling to bits, but I think I have managed to give the end of the picture an uplift that was sorely needed.

TWO SHOT — LYDIA AND MELANIE
*On the back seat. Melanie begins sobbing in a sudden
release of tension. Lydia, in compassion, and tenderly,
cradles Melanie's head on her shoulder. Melanie, her
eyes glistening, looks ahead through the windshield.*

FULL SHOT — THE CAR INTERIOR
All their faces visible.

CATHY

Mitch? Do . . . do you think the lovebirds will
be all right? In the trunk? Can they breathe?

MITCH
(with the faintest smile)

I think they'll be all right, honey.

*There is hope on their faces as the car streaks into the
wind. Not a wild exuberance, but a relaxation of tension.
They stare ahead through the windshield, and then they
squint their eyes against the sudden sunrise ahead, and
Mitch reaches up to turn down the sun visor.*

It looks . . . it looks clear up ahead.

FULL SHOT — THE CAR
*Moving away from the camera fast into the magnificent
sunrise over the crest of the hills. Further and further
into the distance it goes.*

FADE OUT

THE END

'I think this does the trick,' I wrote, 'but since there
is still time before you shoot this scene, please let me

know if anything about it troubles you.'

It was all a pointless exercise. Cooler heads were about to prevail.

Not a week had gone by before Hitch fired off the new script to his good old pal, V. S. Pritchett. I never saw the letter of April 9, in which he asked Pritchett to add to an earlier scene in the film the information that, when Melanie was a young girl, her mother had run off with another man. Toward that end, and to reinforce this pointless piece of exposition, he suggested that the moment the convertible top shreds away Melanie should fight her way out of Lydia's embrace and shout something like, 'Let me out! Let me go back! Mother, I want you, I want you. Come back to me, please – please come back to me.'

I suppose I should be grateful that the final scene in the car was never shot. Otherwise those lines would have been attributed to me as the writer who received sole screenplay credit. To Mr Pritchett, however, must go the credit (or blame) for urging that the film end on a gloomier note, with the people in the car 'looking backwards at the village with fear, rather than forward to the hope of escape'. (You will remember that in my first draft, Mitch Brenner expressed the fear that the birds *might* be in San Francisco when they got there.) But it was Pritchett's suggestion that translated itself into what became the final scene of the film.

When I saw the movie for the first time at the Museum of Modern Art's invitational screening a year later – and realized that Hitch had sacrificed my ending in favor of what he called 'the most difficult shot' he'd ever done, a composite of birds requiring thirty-two separate exposures against a matte painting – I was appalled. The very hip and sophisticated black-tie audience was, to say the very least, somewhat glacially polite in its reception. A stunned silence greeted the final complicated mosaic of what appeared to be 3,407 pieces of bird film. Later, when I saw the movie in a commercial theatre, people actually turned to each other and mumbled, 'Is it over? Is that it? Huh?' I left before they realized I was the man who'd written the screenplay and mistakenly assumed the ending they had just seen had been concocted by me.

Hitch later said that he hadn't filmed my last pages because he felt they were superfluous. 'Emotionally speaking,' he said, 'the movie was already over for the audience. The additional scenes would have been playing while everyone was leaving their seats and walking up the aisles.'

No.

Hitch didn't film the scene I wrote because then he would have made a movie with a thrilling, suspenseful ending.

He wasn't going for that.

He was going for high art.

April 20, 1962

Dear Hitch:

Just a short note to tell you that *Marnie* is moving along nicely. I now have about ninety polished pages with only one possible problem in sight: that of length.

I am delighted with the way all the characters (even the minor ones) are shaping up. I hope you are having as much fun with our little feathered friends.

May 7, 1962

Dear Hitch:

Anita and I returned last night from a long weekend in Puerto Rico, and today I reread the screenplay to date and made some minor additions and corrections. It was good getting away from it for a few days because it allowed me the opportunity of seeing it in a fresh light. I must say I am absolutely delighted with the way it is going.

A red-breasted grosbeak, sir, was just sitting outside my study window, tapping at the glass. I told him the picture had already hired its full complement of actors, and was indeed now shooting in LA He turned away with a distinctly hangdog expression.

MITCH

Are they molting now?

MELANIE

Some of them are.

MITCH

How can you tell?

MELANIE

Well . . . they get a sort of hangdog expression.

CLOSE SHOT – A CAGED BIRD – MITCH'S POV
The bird is wearing a distinctly hangdog expression.

I must have delivered the first draft of *Marnie* sometime around the middle of June. My records show that I was paid for the week of June 11, 1962 and that there was not another weekly salary check until December 10, 1962. I feel certain I went to the Coast shortly after Hitch read the script. He was still wrapping up *The Birds* and had yet to film what turned out to be the last big attack, the famous (or infamous, depending on one's point of view) attic scene, during which he hurled live bird after bird at his inexperienced, bewildered, and ultimately terrified actress.

One morning, Roy Taylor came to me.
'Did you write this scene?' he asked, and handed me some pages . . .
I read the scene.
It takes place on a hill above the Brenner house, just prior to the bird attack on the children's birthday party. Melanie and Mitch are alone. Miraculously, he has a martini pitcher and long-stemmed martini glasses with him. He pours, they drink. Then Melanie pours out her heart.

MITCH
You need a mother's care, my child!

MELANIE
Not my mother's!

68

MITCH

Oh – I'm sorry.

MELANIE

What have you got to be sorry about? My
mother? Don't waste your time. She ditched us
when I was eleven and went off with some
hotel man in the east. You know what a
mother's love is?

MITCH

Yes, I do.

MELANIE

You mean it's better to be ditched?

MITCH

No, I think it's better to be loved. Don't you
ever see her?

MELANIE

(*turning away to hide the tears*)
I don't know where she is.
(*recovering her composure*)
Well! Maybe I ought to go join the *other*
children.

I was happy to tell Rod I had definitely *not* written
that scene, and had not in fact seen those pages until
the moment he'd handed them to me.

'Well, we're shooting it this morning,' he said.

Over my dead body, I thought, and went to find
Hitch.

He was in the production trailer with Peggy. I

asked if I might talk to him privately, and then showed him the scene Rod had given me. I said I didn't know who'd written it but that it was totally inept and devoid of any craftsmanship, that no single speech in it logically followed the speech preceding it, that a first-year film student at UCLA could write a better scene, and that I would be thoroughly embarrassed if it were to appear in a movie with my name on it as screenwriter.

Hitch did his straight-faced little take.

Then he said, 'Are you going to trust me or a two-bit actor?'

They shot the scene that morning.

It is in the picture.

I later learned that Hitch himself had written it.

I remember sitting with him in a darkened screening room and watching the unassembled dailies of the attic attack. 'Hurry up, hurry up' he yelled between each frantic take. 'Hurry up' he yelled, while makeup people bloodied Tippi's face and hands, and wardrobe people tore her clothes, and The Girl genuinely cowered in fear of each new assault.

A letter to my then agent, Scott Meredith, explains my mood later that summer:

Dear Scott,

I guess this postponement of *Marnie* has affected me harder than I realized at first.

I had planned to have the final screenplay completed by August, as you know, take the trip to

Europe for a month (which I think I sorely need after what amounts to a full year of working on screenplays and mysteries) and then begin work on the law novel in September. Frankly, I was looking forward to the luxury of turning off everything but the telephone and beginning work on a book that is certainly long overdue from everyone's standpoint, including my own. The postponement of *Marnie* presents a dilemma, and I frankly don't know what to do about it.

I know very well that I can fill the time before leaving for Europe by doing another McBain novelette, or even by writing a television play for one of those cockamamie outfits that have been bugging us, or I can sit and pick lint from my navel, but none of these projects will change the simple facts. Those facts are: Hitchcock *will* be back sooner or later, ready to work on the script, and *I* will have to postpone or interrupt work on a novel in progress.

I think we both agreed a long time ago that the surest way to get sandtrapped into all this Hollywood crap was to undertake one screenplay immediately after another. I don't buy the Hollywood Corruption idea except as a corruption of reality, and somehow or other we have slipped into screenplay, screenplay, screenplay – and this, Scott, *is* a corruption of reality. I am a novelist. If one more columnist calls me 'screenwriter Evan Hunter' I think I'll climb the wall.

We will see what happens. After all this ranting and raving, we always get down to that: we will see what happens. I am not being petulant about the interruption of a work schedule that seemed important to me. I am simply expressing the heartfelt desire that once, just once, I can plan my own time and fill it exactly as I want to. I once had the mistaken childish notion that this was what made writing attractive.

November 7, 1962

Dear Hitch:

I have been informed by the Meredith office that you'll be ready to resume work on *Marnie* on the 26th of this month. That should give me enough time to clear up some odds and ends, and I'll be looking forward to seeing you.

Christmas was fast approaching, and I was in California.

I had not yet bought gifts for any of my family; my daily conferences on *Marnie* left me exhausted and hardly in the mood for shopping in a climate where Santa Claus and Christmas trees seemed anomalous. I wanted to go back to New York.

One afternoon, Hitch was telling me a long story about Charles Laughton and the shooting of *Jamaica Inn*, an anecdote I might have otherwise found fascinating – but I was getting impatient. I interrupted him mid-sentence.

'Excuse me, Hitch,' I said, 'but do you know what my salary is?'

'I know it's exorbitant,' he said.

Our private joke.

'Then shouldn't we get back to discussing *Marnie*?'

He looked at me blankly.

Somehow it wasn't quite his usual classic take.

'Of course,' he said.

Later that afternoon, Lew Wasserman, Universal's chief executive and Hitch's former agent and long-time friend, stopped by the office to chat. He'd been with us for about five minutes when Hitch interrupted *him* mid-sentence.

'Excuse me, Lew,' he said, 'but we'll have to cut this short. Mr *Hunter* is eager to get home for Christmas.'

I know I was home again for Christmas, and I know I was back in Los Angeles again on February 4, 1963 because that was when Hitch and I sat down with a tape recorder and Bob Boyle.

Bit by bit, scene by scene, just as I had done for him every morning while we were shaping the screenplay for *The Birds*, just as I had done for Peggy Robertson every afternoon of the working process, Hitch *himself* now told the complete story of *Marnie*, explaining what we would be doing in every scene. I interrupted occasionally – to clarify a point, to add something that may have slipped his mind – but for the most part, this was Hitch's recitation, and his grasp of the movie was encyclopedic. For the most part, Bob and I merely listened.

'The cabin of the ship has to be a bedroom and a sitting room, a suite,' he said into the recorder's microphone. 'And she's in a negligee. He's in shirt and pants. And he comes over to embrace her now.

73

The primal scene: Sean Connery confronts Tippi Hedren.

Now is the moment. And she turns on him and walks away and sits in a far corner of the sitting room . . .

'And then you get the second night in the cabin. He comes to her and she tries to resist – and then she turns her head away and you follow her head as he forces her down onto the bed, and you know . . . '

He turned off the machine.

And described Marnie's rape in detail.

I was the new kid on the block, and still learning the ways of the world. But I knew better than to contradict the boss in the presence of a man with whom he'd begun working twenty years earlier.

I took Hitch aside later.

I told him that I did not want to write that scene as he had outlined it. I told him we would lose all sympathy for the male lead if he rapes his own wife on their honeymoon. I told him we can see the girl isn't being coy or modest, she's terrified, she's trembling, and the reasons for this all come out in the later psychiatric sessions. I told him if the man really loved her he would take her in his arms and comfort her gently and tell her they'd work it out, don't be frightened, everything will be all right. I told him that's how *I* thought the scene should go.

Hitch held up his hands the way directors do when they're framing a shot. Palms out, fingers together, thumbs extended and touching to form a perfect square. Moving his hands toward my face, like a camera coming in for a close shot, he said,

Hitchcock framing the shot for Connery and Hedren.

'Evan, when he sticks it in her, I want that camera right on her *face!*'

Many years later, when I told Jay Presson Allen how much his description of that scene had bothered me, she said, 'You just got bothered by the scene that was his reason for making the movie. You just wrote your ticket back to New York.'

It was on that same trip that Hitch revealed the advertising slogan he wanted to use on *The Birds*.

For the unveiling of it, he assembled in his office all of Universal's marketing people. I hadn't heard the slogan before. It was to be a surprise to me as well.

'Gentlemen,' he said, 'here's how we'll announce the movie. Are you ready?'

There was a moment of suspenseful silence, the master at work. Spreading his hands wide on the air, Hitch said, '*The Birds* is coming!'

It was pure genius, a seemingly ungrammatical catchphrase that combined humor and suspense.

One of Universal's young advertising Turks said, 'Excuse me, Mr Hitchcock, sir?'

Hitch turned to him.

'Don't you mean "The birds *are* coming", sir?'

'The Girl wants the *mink*,' Hitch said.

The Girl was Tippi Hedren. The mink was the one Melanie Daniels, The Girl in the picture, wore throughout the filming.

'So give it to her,' I said.

'Do you know how much that coat *costs*?' he asked.

'You can afford it,' I said.

We sat alone in the screening room, side by side, Hitch and I, watching the opening credits of the film. He had decided by then that there would be no score for *The Birds*. Unmindful of his artistic pretensions for the film, I told him I thought that would be a mistake, that music could subtly foreshadow dire events to come or stridently accompany bird attacks until we had the audience screaming. He said no. No music.

The titles had no music behind them.

The screen was filled with fuzzy images of flying birds. There was the sound of wings whirring. There was the sound of birds squeaking and eeking. It was all very scary and portentous. Maybe he was right.

By various agreements among writers, directors and production companies, the last three credits to appear before any movie actually begins are Producer, Writer, Director, in that order. Which writer or writers will get screen credit is determined by the Writers Guild. If a writer is entitled to *sole* screenplay credit, he will receive it on a separate card with no other name appearing on it. The size of the credit is related to the main title. Fifty per cent of the title, sixty per cent, whatever.

I was the sole writer on *The Birds* and entitled to credit on a separate card. Following my credit was Du Maurier's 'Based on' credit. Then came Hitch's 'Directed by' credit. It was one hundred per cent of the title.

He waited until all the credits had run out.

In the dark, he called, 'How big is Evan's name?'

A voice from the projection booth called, 'Twenty-five per cent, sir.'

'Raise it to fifty,' he said.

Guilt-stricken, I hoped.

'I sometimes wonder what the point of it is,' he once told me. 'A hundred years from now, it'll all be cornflakes in the can.'

February 25, 1963

Dear Peggy:

Thank you for the material on the glassworks, which was exactly what I needed for the *Marnie* factory background. I am now lacking the technical information for the conversation between the exhibitor and the projectionist. I hope you will be sending that along soon.

I am very pleased with the way the script is going, and my only modest desire is that the movie will become another testimonial to the greatness of the man who wrote the novel. Please give my warmest regards to Hitch.

Best wishes . . .

February 27, 1963

Dear Peggy:

A friend of mine at *Revue* sent me two yellow car stickers proclaiming 'The birds is coming.' I have promptly stuck one on my car and one on Anita's, but since my friends in New York are legion, can you send me a dozen more so that I can have them plastered onto additional cars?

When *is* the birds coming?

Best wishes . . .

March 1, 1963

Dear Evan:

In accordance with our customary prompt and efficient method, we are – at this very moment – air-mailing to you one dozen 'the birds is coming' stickers to be plastered on your personal fleet of automobiles.

Also, at this very moment, Hitch is telephoning you with the details of when the birds is coming.

Enclosed please find copy of a letter written to our research department from Steuben Glass (for

Hitchcock publicizing *The Birds.*

your personal information) together with a copy of notes from another source on the duties of an assistant cashier during her first day at work.

Was very touched by your adulation and concern for Mr Winston Graham.

Best wishes,
Peggy

March 7, 1963

Dear Evan:

This is just a little note to confirm that you and Anita will be my guests at the first special showing of *The Birds* at the Museum of Modern Art Theater on Wednesday, March 27 at 8:30.

Before this, Alma would very much like you to

join us for a libation and a modest repast, in the
Library on the mezzanine floor at the St Regis
Hotel at 6:00.
    Love,
    Hitch

He had closed his letter with the word 'Love' and
had personally signed it 'Hitch'.

                                    March 8, 1963
Dear Evan:
    Herewith the information on the stock transfer.
    Incidentally, it will be definitely 'black tie' at the
Museum of Modern Arts screening of *The Birds*.
    Best wishes,
    Peggy

Peggy's letter to me crossed mine of the same date:

                                    March 8, 1963
Dear Peggy:
    Thank you for the transcript of the dialogue
between the erudite manager of the La Reina
Theater and his garrulous projectionist. Does the
manager always have a tiny microphone concealed
on him, or was he fitted especially for the job? All I
have to say is that even with a super cinephor lens, it
was difficult to flatten out this marathon discourse.
    Thank you, too, for the information on an
assistant cashier's duties. I see no mention here of
what her attitude toward partners of the company
should be and I am at a total loss trying to reconcile

these facts with the behaviour of Marnie/Terry, Marnie/Mark. Would you please contact Steuben Glass (who seem so *very* cooperative) and ask them what an assistant cashier does when the boss begins chasing her around the desk?

I have also received the yellow and black stickers, and have put one on my chauffeur-driven Cadillac, another on my Alfa Romeo, a third on my yacht, a fourth on my Piper Cub, and one on each of my skis. The other night, while taking a shower, Anita suggested that I stick one on my . . . but I digress.

As you can tell from my jovial mood, I am delighted with the way the script is going, and I am looking forward to the black tie preview of *The Birds*. My garbage man has promised to lend me his tuxedo, and I will be buying a new pair of saddle shoes especially for the occasion.

If you need me, darling, I will fly to your side immediately.

Passionately . . .

March 12, 1963

Dear Evan:

It was with deep regret that I learned that you are not completely satisfied with the dialogue between the manager of La Reina Theater and his projectionist. I hereby promise that I will divulge nothing when I find this dialogue, in its entirety, inserted in the script.

Now, while I am on this subject, it is timorously and with great hesitation that I feel it obligatory to draw to your attention yet another of those errors with which I am constantly being tormented! i.e. in the first sentence of your letter when you refer to '. . . the manager of the La Reina Theater'. The translation of the words 'La Reina' is 'The Queen'. Now let me put this in a way that you will understand.

When you say 'the manager of the La Reina Theater', you are actually saying 'the manager of the the Queen Theater'. No, please do not thank me for this lesson. The fact that I am able to rectify even one small mark of illiteracy is reward enough.

With regard to my research on secretaries being chased around desks by their bosses – may I suggest that you contact your own secretary. I have checked Sue and Joan but they are too shy to report on their volitations from you.

Have something to eat before you start (for *The Birds* preview). I'd feel a lot better.'

With devotion from the President of the Le Evan Hunter Fan Club, I am

Yours Truly . . .

Peggy's reference to having something to eat was from the scene following the bird attack on the children's birthday party.

> MELANIE
> Mitch . . . what's happening?

> MITCH
> (*concerned*)
> I don't know, Melanie.
> (*pause*)

Look, do you have to go back to Annie's?

MELANIE

No, I have my things in that car.

MITCH
(*gently*)
Then stay and have something to eat before
you start back. I'd feel a lot better.

I myself wrote these memorable lines for that
unfortunate actor to say, transforming him in the
wink of an eye from a heroic leading man to a
concerned Jewish mother. Aside from the scene on
the hill, which Hitch himself wrote, these are the
worst lines in the movie. He was unable to edit them
out because they were spoken in a close shot and he
had no covering footage. Of course they became the
butt of a continuing dialogue between Peggy and
me. This jovial banter was the tenor of the corre-
spondence between us before I delivered the final
draft of *Marnie*. It was then that dear Peggy was
elected to become Hitch's hatchet man.

Hatchet woman.

Okay, hatchet *person*.

Like a fool rushing in, I delivered what I hoped
would be the final draft of *Marnie* on the day after
April Fool's Day. Coincidentally, I had delivered the
final draft of *The Birds* on that same date a year
earlier. What goes around comes around. My letter
accompanying *Marnie* read:

April 2, 1963

Dear Hitch:

Here is *Marnie*, which I believe has shaped up very well. There are a few things I would like to call to your attention, however, since they are deviations from the story as we discussed it. I found that some of our story line simply would not work in the writing, and I adjusted the screenplay accordingly.

The major change I have made concerns the honeymoon night. You will notice that there are two versions of this sequence in the script, one in white, one in yellow. The yellow version is the sequence as we discussed it, complete with the poolside scene and the rape. I wrote and rewrote and polished and repolished this sequence, but something about it continued to disturb me. I finally wrote the white version – which is the version *I would like to see in the film*.

I know you are fond of the entire honeymoon sequence as we discussed it, Hitch, but let me tell you what I felt was wrong with it, and how I attempted to bring it into a truer perspective.

To begin with, Marnie's attitude was misleading. We were asking an audience to believe that putting off Mark was on her mind from the top of the scene. This makes her frigidity a cold-blooded thing (no pun intended) rather than something she cannot help. She *can* respond to warmth and gentleness, she *can* accept love-making – until it gets serious. Which brings us to a further examination. WHY *DOES* MARNIE MARRY HIM?

The answer is simple: she loves him. She may think she is marrying him to avoid the police, but she really does love him (as we bring out at the picture's end). It is only her deep emotional disturbance that makes it impossible for her to accept his love.

I have, therefore, written a rather playful honeymoon night scene, showing Marnie in a gay and likable mood, a bit giggly (we have never seen her this way in the picture before), playing our entire Garrod's exposition as a warm love scene, which I think works. It is only when Mark's intentions get serious, only when his love-making reminds her of that night long ago, that she panics and pulls away. Her retreat is a curious thing and the audience – for the first time – realizes that something is seriously wrong with this girl. The scene is frightening, and it also provides a springboard for the later scene in which Mark suggests psychiatric help. To me, it is believable and sound. The way we discussed it was implausibility bordering on burlesque.

Which brings us to the second major change.

In the yellow version, I have done the rape sequence as we discussed it. In the white version, I have eliminated it entirely. *I firmly believe it is out of place in this story.* Mark is *not* that kind of a person; Marnie is obviously troubled, and he realizes it. Stanley Kowalski might rape her, but *not* Mark Rutland. Mark would do exactly what we see him do later on – he would seek the help of a psychiatrist. And, without an out-of-character rape, there was no need for a poolside discussion. The entire honeymoon sequence now takes place on a single night. Marnie's panic is followed immediately by her suicide attempt. There is no long stage wait. I am convinced that the rape has no place in this sequence, Hitch, and I hope you will agree and throw away the yellow pages.

I will be waiting to hear from you, and expecting to come West whenever you say.

You just got bothered by the scene that was his reason for making the movie. You just wrote your ticket back to New York.

There were no fax machines or express mail systems in those days. I had sent off the script by air mail special delivery. Even assuming Hitch received it on the Coast only two days later – an optimistic assumption for 1963 – it did not take long for him to get back to me. His return letter was dated April 10, 1963. It read:

Dear Evan,
I have been through the script and feel there is still a lot of work to be done on it.

Unfortunately, I feel that I have gone stale on it and think it will have to be put aside for a little while until I can decide what to do about it. It may be it needs a fresh mind altogether, and this probably will have to be the next procedure.

I'm sorry I couldn't give you any better news than this, but there it is; and as I said above, it is

87

going to need still a lot of work to get it into condition that will satisfy me.

Kindest regards,
Alfred J. Hitchcock

His signature was rubber-stamped.

I knew very well what he meant by 'a fresh mind altogether' but I chose to be deliberately obtuse in my return letter, which was dated April 15.

Dear Hitch:

Since *Marnie* has been virtually the sole interest of my creative life since February of last year, I am understandably surprised and disappointed by your reaction to the screenplay. This is particularly true in view of the fact that I feel the script is a faithful and honestly realized rendering of all we discussed on the Coast.

Certainly any problems which may exist in the script can be remedied after discussion. And perhaps some of these will be found to be less grave than they now appear once the situation you mention, your temporary feeling of staleness toward the project, has been overcome.

I do agree completely that it would be a good idea to put the project aside until we can both return to it with fresh minds. I imagine this will be when you've completed the remaining promotional work on *The Birds*. But *whenever* you're ready, I'll do my utmost, as always, to stop work at once on other projects so that we may complete *Marnie* to

our mutual satisfaction. It goes without saying that
this project, in addition to any business
considerations, has come to mean a great deal to
me personally.

My very best wishes . . .

*Evan, when he sticks it in her, I want that camera right
on her face!*

On the first day of May, Peggy Robertson called my
agent to say that I was being replaced on the picture
by another writer.

I felt no joy when *Marnie* opened to dreadful
reviews.

Sometime after that, I was on the Coast again
with Anita, and I called Hitch's office to ask if he
and Alma would care to join us for dinner. Peggy
called back an hour or so later to say they would be
delighted.

We were staying at the Beverly Wilshire; we asked
them to meet us in the dining-room there.

It was as if nothing uncomfortable had ever
passed between us.

Hitch was his usual entertaining, anecdotal,
expansive, droll, mischievous, witty self. At one
point, he told me that someday he wanted to shoot
an entire film *behind* the scenes in New York. If we
played a scene at Le Circe, it would not be in the
dining-room, but in the kitchen. If we played a scene
at the Eugene O'Neill Theater, it would not be in the
audience or on the stage, but in the wings. If we

played a scene at the Empire State Building, it would not be on the observation tower but in the basement.

'Maybe you'll write it for me, hm?' he said.

Anita was telling Alma that our room was somewhat cheerless, and that she was thinking of ordering some flowers for it.

Hitch beckoned to Hernando Courtwright, who then owned the hotel. Patting Anita's hand, Hitch asked, 'Don't you think it would be nice if Mrs Hunter had some *flowers* in her room?'

When Anita and I went back upstairs later that evening, the room was blooming everywhere.

That was a long time ago.

It is sad to think there will never again be another Hitchcock film. Every time I publish a new novel, I wonder if it is something Hitch might care to film, something I myself might adapt for him.

Screenplay by Evan Hunter, based on his novel.
Directed by Alfred Hitchcock.

I would settle for twenty-five per cent of the title

Hitchcock's cameo appearance in the first scene of *The Birds*.